Illumen
Winter 2020

In this issue:

Featured Poet: E. P. Fisher

The Francis W. Alexander Interview

The JD DeHart Page

Article: Review of FJ Bergmann's
A Catalog of the Further Suns

Alban Lake Publishing

Illumen
Winter 2020
Edited by Tyree Campbell

All rights reserved. No part of this book may be reproduced or transmitted in any form or by any means, electronic or mechanical, including photocopying or recording or by any information storage and retrieval systems, without expressed written consent of the author and/or artists.

Illumen is a work of fiction. Names, characters, places, and incidents are products of the author's imagination. Any resemblance to actual events or persons, living or dead, is entirely coincidental.

Story copyrights owned by Kyle McKeon
Cover art "Sarrow Sees" by Betharyelle Taylor
Cover design by Karen Otto

First Printing
January 2020

Alban Lake Publishing
P.O. Box 141
Colo, Iowa 50056-0141 USA
e-mail: albanlake@yahoo.com

Visit www.albanlakepublishing.com for online science fiction, fantasy, horror, scifaiku, and more. Stop by our online bookstore at www.irbstore.co for novels, magazines, anthologies, and collections. Support the small, independent press and your First Amendment rights.

Available at *www.irbstore.com*, at Barnes and Noble, and on Amazon.com!

Or just use the order form at the back of this book!

A Little Help, Please

In the world of the small indie press we fight a never-ending battle for attention to our work, as writers and in publishing. Here's an example: big publishers [you know who they are] have gobs of $$$ that they can devote to advertising and marketing. Here at Alban Lake, our advetising budget consists of the deposits for whatever soda bottles and aluminum cans we can find alongside the highways. Anti-littering laws make our task even more difficult... ☺

That's where YOU come in. YOU are our best promoter. YOU are the one who can tell others about us. Just send 'em to our website, tell them about our store. That's all. Just that.

Of course, we don't mind if you talk us up. We're pretty good, you know. We have some award-winning and award-nominated writers and artists, plus other voices well-deserving to be heard [not everyone wins awards, right?] but our publications are read-worthy nevertheless.

That number once again is:
www.albanlakepublishing.com

Friend us on Facebook at
　　　Alban Lake Publishing
Follow us on Twitter at
　　　@albanlake and @albanlakepub

Contents

Features

4	Review of FJ Bergmann's *A Catalog of the Further Suns*, by Daniel C. Smith
22	A Day in the Life Interview Series: Francis W. Alexander, with Terrie Leigh Relf
37	Featured Poet: E. P. Fisher
43	The JD DeHart Page
56	Who's Who

Poems

1	At Play Down Dark Lane by Claire Smith
2	Ocean Tales by Stephanie Smith
3	To the Quarry by Oliver Smith
9	Memento Mori by Jen Sexton-Riley
10	Cicada Summer by Christen Leah
12	The Robo-Child, Now Available in the One-Year-Old Model by John Grey
14	Sleeps Beneath the Streets by Simon Kewin
15	The Day the Internet Went Away by Debby Feo
17	Gods of Winter by Brian Rosenberger
18	What's It All About by Rachel Rodman
19	Darkness by Rachel Rodman
20	Nightmare City by Stephanie Smith
21	The Bean Sidhe of *Uí Briúin Clan* by Deborah Guzzi
34	On Xereon by John Grey
36	Choosing a Mate by John Grey
44	Running Away by Roger Singer
45	Cherry Wine by Avra Margariti

46	afterlife by Peter Roberts
47	Rue d'Auseil by DJ Tyrer
49	Witch Night by DJ Tyrer
50	The City Built on Ashes by Edward Hickcox
52	Virgo's in Valhalla by Deborah Guzzi
53	Origami by Brian Rosenberger
55	A Wolf Walks into a Bar by Avra Margariti

What? No subscription to Illumen?

We can fix that...

Just go here and order:

https://www.irbstore.co/product-page/illumen-subscription

Or use the order form at the back of this book!

At Play Down Dark Lane
Claire Smith

On a Summer Solstice night, curious,
they wound their way down a deserted track.
The sun sank, lower, in the dusky sky.
Its warmth ebbed, vanished, and flowed away.

The pair reached the bottom of the trail,
saw a black cat stretched on the moist grass;
green eyes flashed against the dark
stared at the two children, steady, intense.

The sign, *Salem Cottage,* was half-buried
in a mound of grass by a broken wall.
The place tempted the pair forward, onwards,
ready: to trespass, to peek, to eavesdrop.

Invited to look in mildewed windows
rotten frames home to woodlice and earwigs.
Filthy glass panes hiding places for spiders
to spin their webs, wait for unsuspecting flies.

They saw their chance to play *Knock down Ginger.*
Banged on the front door, raced back to blend
in with roadside bushes; they hid where night
kisses brambles, stinging nettles, ferns.

Hungry laughter: savoured, tasted, salivated,
the promise of delicacies long deprived.
Caught the two, hidden, revealed by dawn;
cut apart and served up by the rising sun.

Edited by Tyree Campbell

Ocean Tales
Stephanie Smith

At the bottom of the ocean
swims my stagnant memory
A little fish with human teeth
that dreams of devouring the world

There are things that I remember, still
Places I've seen. Shapes that I've been,
morphing through time and space
Maybe I am still these things
A country all my own

I am an island rising to the sky
with a giant mouth and bloodshot eyes

I am a lonely castaway,
allergic to coconuts, yet unafraid

I am the laughter
of the children we once were,
as precious as the pirate's treasure
lost forever on the ocean floor

To the Quarry
Oliver Smith

The scree road snakes through grey boulders
crumbs from the quarry bitten from the hill
long abandoned to erosion,
hidden under raven's bones, and dove nests
he could ascend by any of the thirteen paths
that zig-zag up its broken face.

His destination: a thin stream that trickles
from a cave a hundred feet up;
they found the ancient mirror here
and trapped in its bronze surface
he saw a reflection without a face:
a mask enclosed by Time.

They said this path led nowhere
now he reaches the door
high up in the yellow stone
that will take him, so far beyond
home, to the golden stars.
When he sits on that threshold
and looks down on the Earth
there are rocks, woods, plains, hills,
the last horizon waiting
and bleached in the flux
of an already alien sun.

Edited by Tyree Campbell

A Catalog of the Further Suns by FJ Bergmann: A Review
Daniel C. Smith

The world of speculative literature certainly suffers no lack of poets, yet too much of the poetry produced within the genre often lacks—*dare I say it?*—gravity. The poetic elements that constitute the great works of our collective canon are often absent, or worse, treated as afterthought. Occasionally though, someone will break orbit with an offering that embodies the best qualities of both poetry and speculative literature while elevating the art of poetry of the fantastic at the same time. Such is the case with FJ Bergmann's *A Catalogue of the Further Suns*, a collection of previously published poems culled from some of science fiction's most acclaimed venues, all related by a thematic arc (think concept album) exploring sci-fi's most classic themes—deep space exploration and contact with extraterrestrials. Poetry allows us to experience the so-called human condition through emotion and imagery, and what better way to explore what it means to be human than by consideration of our possible effect upon alien species and cultures? Or, just as important, their effect upon us? Exercising both an eloquence and an economy with words, Bergmann takes the reader beyond those most distant stars on a revealing sojourn that bridges the gulf between the known and the unknown, the human and the inhumane. For instance, the line

"...they permitted no embellishments to lard their lean truths... "

from *Xenoaesthetics* not only provides a wellspring of information with regards to an alien culture, it is also perhaps indicative of Bergmann's stylistic approach—at least with regards to this particular body of work.

Lines such as these slice through layers of skin, peeling back tendons and sinew with an elegant precision and cutting to the bone, exposing the bare and often unpleasant truths of our own existence while exploring our impact upon one another through the lens of the 'other'. Bergmann's delivery—a blunt honesty similar to the hard-hitting pull no punches style of, say, Sandra Cisneros or the late Jim Carroll—allows for a fresh and creative exploration of what made classic science fiction 'classic'. The motifs brandished within these prose-styled lines are certainly familiar enough to the fans of the speculative genres, from post-apocalyptic, glaciated wastelands, aboriginal cultures and completely alien yet eerily familiar landscapes. However, all of this would not have as much impact without Bergmann's knack for employing what I think of as 'the 'implied', whereas in fiction we try to show as oppose to tell, I believe that an important skill of the best poets is the ability to imply as opposed to show. My own favorite example of this is the last line of Yeats poem about vampires "Oil and Blood":

"*Their shrouds are bloody and their lips are wet.*"

It has been a busy night for the now satiated pieces of darkness, resting after a feast about

Edited by Tyree Campbell

which Yeats allowed our imaginations to fill in the blank spaces, implication being a stronger emotive device rather gory detail. Now consider the last few lines from *Xaphiaarchy*, a stark depiction of a race of hunter-warriors:

" *...until the moment*
when their prey knelt in despair to offer
a shuddering throat to the blade..."

Obviously these folks aren't just hunting animals. These sparse, lean lines show us something essentially revealing about their character and the brutal nature of life on their world, not told or demonstrated, but implicated by the words not written. This quality is again best demonstrated in *Pavane*, a truly horrific portrait of a unique cultural paradigm whereupon the hour of a subject's demise is predetermined and super-imposed by self-anointed authority:

"*...secret cults devoted to making the demise*
of others diverge completely from times
and circumstances foretold..."

Again the power of implication is enough to allow the reader to understand that, in this society, on this world, rebellion and it's resulting chaos mean murder. This adeptness, alongside more than a few other unique skill palettes accessible to only a select number of poets, all allowing Bergmann to achieve, within the medium of poetry, the scope of Space Opera. *A Catalog of the Furthest Suns* is a path of suggestions and subtleties like whispy and decaying ion trails—left behind from who knows who or what?—that can be followed into uncharted territory by those who dare to find destinations that stir the consciousness as well as the conscience. Tackling (head on) some tough social issues regarding the exploration and 'colonization' of new worlds; the closest parallel that I can draw within more contemporary literature is Dee Brown's *Bury My Heart at Wounded Knee*, a recitation of early American colonial history as told from the viewpoint of Native Americans. We have all heard the phrase 'history is written by the victors'—but history reads very differently through the eyes of the displaced and the dispossessed, those cultures considered 'lesser' due to a lack of gadgetry or economic competition. *Further Suns* challenges the reader to ask if history will repeat itself as we expand our reach into outer space. Will the men and women who walk on, say, *Tau Ceti Four*, be any wiser or kinder than the colonists who landed at *Plymouth Rock*? An especially poignant question considering at this very moment the United States seems to be hell-bent for leather on militarizing near-Earth orbit and beyond. Perhaps history is already repeating itself, perhaps we are what we are, unable to change. I for one would like to believe that we have more to offer the universe than our germs, petty aggression's and our snobbery towards culture 'less advanced'—an all too often overlooked form of bigotry.

  Meanwhile, *A Catalogue of the Further Suns* is both an introspective and interstellar journey well worth taking. Available from Amazon.com as well as directly from the publisher, Gold Line Press, at <www.spdbooks.org>, or <800.869.7553>.

Edited by Tyree Campbell

Out on their first date, high school seniors Colo Collins and Tama Toledo are taken aboard a spaceship and offered the chance to intervene in various events in the Universe. These events can range from stopping an asteroid from striking a planet to helping someone find her house keys. But there's a catch: both Colo and Tama have to agree that an intervention should be performed... and sometimes they'll have to perform the intervention themselves!

Available at www.irbstore.com, at Barnes and Noble, and on Amazon.com!

Or just use the order form at the back of this book!

Memento Mori
Jen Sexton-Riley

What was it the monster said
Out of reach of the nightlight
   under my bed?

What song did the boneman gently plink
When the piano tempted him
   under the sink?

The bats and the shades
   and the girl on my roof
What was their one enduring truth?

I used to know.
I forgot 'til today.
Now it's all coming back
   and so are they.

Edited by Tyree Campbell

Cicada Summer
Christen Leah

Cicada shells, I'm familiar with
My sister showed me
They stuck to the tree like they'd been glued

And you, you've seen them too
Fragile little things
Echoes of the eleven-year swarm

It warms my heart to think of you
Pointing to them in fascination
As though they were trinkets

You loved them
Like they were tokens
That bought you the summer

Wooden Nickels I call them
Too good to be true
So very much like you

I know I care too much
About such trivial matters
But you see the invisible

Value in the exoskeleton
Beauty in nature's fridge magnets
That which I take for granted

Because I have to say
And I mean this in the best possible way
Summer is abysmal

When the mosquitoes are medically certified
They come to draw my blood
But they miss the vein and keep on trying

Then those red cross volunteers are dying
Splattered to smithereens
Bloody little bugs dead on my thighs
And I eulogize, not the bugs
Rather time, give an epitaph
For the days before I was a Pollock

Grotesque in color and form
A canvas of regret
Washing away the grime but never the sting

Just a week more of the dog days
Til autumn harvest begins
And plucks me from the root of my misery

I hate to think of you, sunshine
Hibernating with everything else
While I go out and live again

The Robo-Child, Now Available in the One-Year-Old Model
John Grey

It has the virtue of strong metallic cheekbones.
They're painted pink, appear fragile
but are of the toughest elements,
keep the face in line
with stretched but flexible skin
of the finest most human-like materials.

No human womb-like worry.
Perfection is guaranteed.
And they're programmed to always be
on their best behavior.

No, they will not grow
in the way you understand.
Every year, you'll trade yours in
for a slightly larger, more sophisticated model –
(upgraded vocabulary, improved athletic skills,
even, in the year three model,
a remarkably life-like, though unnecessary,
ability to appear toilet-trained.

Remember, depending on your needs,
these android boys and girls can be adjusted
to demand and give real affection
or to be mere show children
e.g. for politicians running for office,
divas flaunting their motherly instincts
on E TV.

While real kids talk back to their parents.
get into trouble, mess up their futures,
end up as who knows what,
our product will always fulfill the destiny
you've imagined for your progeny.

In years to come,
most of the successful people on the planet
won't be people at all
but our product.
Some could even be ripe for the challenge
of raising actual flesh-and-blood kids.
Our technicians are working on just such a
    likelihood.
I mean what's the optimum life
without a little regret along the way?

Sleeps Beneath the Streets
Simon Kewin

Slumbering under the thrum of the city,
it stirs to dreams of elder days
stretches the lengths of its deep strata
to bellow its subsonic rage

Pushes up green-shoot periscopes
to taste the air of the waking world,
with hastate fronds for tongues, and spies
the lie of the land through flower-head eyes

But tendrils strangled in the tarmac,
are withered to sepia by glyphosate
and crushed by boots and roaring wheels
and mown to ground by the enemy's blades.

Injured, it rages under tower blocks
down beyond the hearing of all clocks,
and shudders with loathing its ancient bones
flexes tree-root fingers to crack open those
stones.

The Day the Internet Went Away
Debby Feo

No one could write
No one could find their way
The Day the Internet Went Away

I had a paper to write, due the next day.
Panic
My son had to get from PA to VA
Driving blind
My sisters couldn't get home
From Grandma's new condo

No maps
Lost in Philly
Three right turns?
Lost
If only it would come back on...

Edited by Tyree Campbell

The entirety of the "A Vow of Blood" story arc collected into one book. Every book, every story, every poem in the story of the vampire Gaius and his family has been collected into this single tome.

"Livia insisted that I no longer prey upon humans, as she did not consider this to be honorable. She thought that I should live only on the blood of animals. She even made me take a vow to that effect, on pain of never seeing her again. I took that vow. Livia had been my only source of human kindness. I could not give her up, now that we had found each other again..."

Available at www.irbstore.com, at Barnes and Noble, and on Amazon.com!

Or just use the order form at the back of this book!

Edited by Tyree Campbell

Gods of Winter
Brian Rosenberger

The November Gods are ghosts.
Dead as a Thanksgiving turkey,
Broken wishbones, just fading memories.
Their time has passed.
The Winter Gods appreciate their sacrifice.

Now is the time to sing Christmas carols,
Light the nine candles of the Menorah, ignite the
 Yule log,
Decorate trees, wrap presents, and most of all,
Wait for snow, wait for the World to turn white.

The Gods of Winter do not wrap presents nor
 decorate trees.
They haven't smiled in centuries.
But snow.
They have been known to shovel snow from their
 home,
High above Midgard. Shovel by the blizzard full.
Homemade shovels, made from the skulls of the
 sons of Ymir,
Shovels capable of making small towns
disappear
 in a single scoop.

Still the Gods of Winter do not smile.
It's their duty, as snow continues to drop.
Believers will tell you The Gods of Winter enjoy
Burying our World, smile or not,
Shovelful after shovelful,
As the citizens of two Worlds,
Long for the Gods of Spring.

What It's All About
Rachel Rodman

The Hokey Pokey.
The #42.
But the Greatest of these is Love.

Edited by Tyree Campbell

Darkness
Rachel Rodman

Once it was cut away, it dove down, as far and as deep as it could possibly go: irretrievable, perhaps, but not exactly lost.

Because, now, whenever you look in that place, where you never grew up--where you couldn't, Never-Never, where you *couldn't*, NEVER-NEVER—everything is still there, still raw and inescapable, and it is as if the intervening years have not happened at all.

Because, now, whenever you stare into the Abyss, there is Peter Pan's shadow, staring back at you.

Nightmare City
Stephanie Smith

Fantasy becomes flesh
The sorrow of midnight unraveling
The crescent moon keeps an eye on things
Graveyards sing grim tunes
For children like me
Not a touch nor a whisper
Befits my startled lips
A secret recipe for immortality
Lies hidden in my cloak
A nightmare city where
Murderers become martyrs
Where the wind carries incantations
On its blackened tongue
That make the dead arise
I become their god, their master,
The flame that descends from the heavens
And burns out the hearts of mortal men
I am one with the water and air
The befouled dirt
Where I rest my weary head

The Bean Sidhe of *Uí Briúin Clan*
Deborah Guzzi

Dusk, harbinger of vaporous night, slinks to jet black in shadow, then runs in rivulets of Prussian blue; see how it puddles, outlining the corpse of cypresses?

Fetid puddles fated for footfall abide in moonlight,
alerting the Bean Sidhe to unwary night-walkers. A coyote's howl laps the hungry wind at the forest's edge.

Beneath the stone bridge's unplumbed depth the water quivers as slithering things with forked tongues coil all about her huddled shape as she shrilly keens beside the river-bed.

Long ago she's laid here with the Laird at end of day. Here she lost herself and unborn child in yonder glade. Tonight, her wail heralds Ui Briúin timely death.

A Day in the Life Interview Series
Francis W. Alexander
with Terrie Leigh Relf

1. What are your writing rituals? How do you prepare your space for these activities?

My best time to write is in the early morning. I aim for five in the morning, which gives me plenty of time to create things. First, I do as much exercising as I can. I usually lift barbells. Then, as I write, I listen to music by Spooky Tooth, Hendrix, The Funkadelic, Procol Harum, and other groups pop, soul, or psychedelic. I have used this ritual since my days in college, and now either listen to YouTube, iTunes, or spin albums on my Crosley record player or listen to my CD's.

When I write my horror poems and tales, I listen to spooky YouTube music such as Tubular Bells (The Exorcist) and Dies Irae ("Day of Wrath", the Shining). When I write science fiction, I listen to YouTube videos like *Twilight Zone* and *One Step Beyond*. Psychedelic music is also played as I write.

2. Within what genres do you write? What intrigues you about these?

I write horror, science fiction, haiku, scifaiku, Christian, and Black Studies. I am fascinated by the future possibilities that each genre holds, be they scary or promising. I am also enthralled by the beauty within each genre. For example, in haiku, many times I can feel and smell things in the poet's moment as if I am there with them. When I think about science fiction, I am enthralled by the ideas of other dimensions and universes. I also think about the possibilities of advanced Kardashev scale civilizations, God, and the mysteries of space.

3. Do you have a day job? If so, how do you balance your creative and work time?

No, I do not have a day job. Most of my time is spent writing. In the spring I have a job scoring papers for NCS Pearson. I am also a tutor although I haven't had any assignments lately.

4. What tips do you have for other writers?

I agree with the advice of many established writers. Be persistent. And write, write, write. Read and study the publications where you want to be published.

In the animal kingdom, some animals have lots of offspring. Some of those offspring won't survive, and some will. My stories and poems are my babies. I'd like for all of them to make it, but they won't. Yet, the more of them I write for publication, the more of them I know will get published.

Also, the more experienced one becomes, the more the opportunities there are to be published. You have to see what kind of material your target magazine likes to publishe, so reading the stories in that publication is also important. Plus, I am always learning techniques as I read other writer's works.

And I urge young writer's to be persistent. There will be some bumps and bruises on the way. You have written your best piece and it gets rejected. Keep sending it out or hold it for the future where you might learn more techniques that you can use to improve it. You might also get other ideas that you can add to the manuscript that could make it much better.

Speaking of improvement. I sometimes find myself reading one of my published works and saying to myself, "I could have done better than that!" There is always room for improvement.

5. What are your thoughts on the creative process in general and your creative process in particular?

Just like genius might be "one percent inspiration and ninety-nine percent perspiration", the same can be said for writing. The way I feel these days, it's definitely ninety-nine percent perspiration. I find that it is not as difficult as it feels at first, once you put yourself into the process and stick to it.

I've read somewhere where everyone has their own universe in their minds. I've always believed this. An idea is like a comet entering a solar system or a meteor entering a planet's atmosphere. The ideas and concepts come to you. And when they don't, I think the writer is like an astronaut going to another planet to get raw materials. The materials (ideas) are right there in front of us. All the writer has to do is reach out and grab them. On another level, I believe the ideas in our universe are planets and systems containing beings having conflicts and drama. What we do is report these events featuring those beings.

6. Where do your ideas come from? What inspires you? Intrigues you?

Some ideas come from my dreams or they hit me early in the morning – making me get up and jot them down. As I mentioned above, I think of my mind as being a universe within itself where many ideas and tales are contained. I also look at the world around me and think of the possibilities for the present and future. I keep up with the latest science news and get ideas from that.

I am mostly inspired by people I know, the great and not so great. In 2007 I was friend requested on MySpace by the singer Jessie J. So, whenever I feel down, listening to her music gets me out of my funk. I am also inspired by knowing what she had to go through to be successful. I am also inspired by authors I know such as Terrie Relf, Lenard Moore, the late August Wilson whose theater group I quit in 1969, Linda Addison, and Marge Simon who was one of my early inspirators in science fiction. Recently I've found out that my distant cousin is author Tannarive Due. I recently watched an episode of the *Outer Limits* and was surprised to see an episode written by her husband Steven Barnes, a writer I remember from the early Yahoo writer's groups. I am also inspired whenever someone has read something of mine and told me they wanted to be a writer like me. This happened when I was on MySpace. The lowest age for a person on MySpace was fourteen at the time and the kid wrote me right when MySpace changed their age policies. So, I don't know if that kid has stayed on the writing track or not. I've since had two gentlemen ask me to be their mentors and that feels good and makes me want to better my craft.

That leads me to a time when I was struggling to be a writer. In the early eighties I lived in this apartment in Detroit's Cass Corridor. There was a kid who wanted to be a writer and told me she was going to be a greater writer than me. I had been a student through a newspaper correspondence course and gave her my materials. I have not been to Detroit in years, the building was torn down and I often wonder if she went after her dream. So, besides the money, having readers, and possibly being an established writer, there is also the thrill of mentoring someone and seeing them become successful. Those are the things that can inspire a writer.

Anything mathematical or religious intrigues me. I am also fascinated by discoveries and other facts archeologists such as Ticia Verveer puts on her twitter and Instagram pages. Actually, anything in history: science (especially astronomy), psychology, religion, mathematics, nature, genealogy and human nature intrigues me.

7. What about upcoming publications? Awards and other accolades?

My drabble collection titled "When the Mushrooms Come" was published by Alban Lake in February. I have stories in the *Anthology of Hate*, and *Fantasy Short Stories Anthology Series Book Two*, and a poem in one of the last issues of *Bloodbond*. My poems are forthcoming in

Scifaikuest, Illumen, and the *Poet Explores the Stars Anthology.* My stories will be in the *Trail of Tears Anthology, Drabble Harvest #13,* and *Alien Dimensions.* I am still feeling great after having been nominated for the 2018 Rhyslings and having an honorable mention in *Drabble Harvest #12: Space Westerns.*

8. What are you working on now?

I am working on some science fiction and horror stories, two book manuscripts, and some poems. I have been working on five books for years and finished three of them. The first book was a science fiction themed tale called *Sons of the Stars* and it was rejected, so I'm going to work some more on it and submit it again. *The Phenoms,* a book about minority superheroes fighting a vampire is still being held for possible publication. I still need to do a lot of research before I finish my genealogy book titled, *The Lineage* about my search for my relatives, and I need to find time to finish Strengthened, my memoir about night terrors. I have been procrastinating about my fifth book submission. It is a book of mostly published haiku and haibun that I am about to send out called I Reckon. I've also been holding on to my children's book manuscript about haiku poet Lenard D. Moore.

9. Where do you see yourself as a writer in five years? Ten?

God willing, I see myself having several books published in five to ten years.

10. What challenges have you faced as a writer and/or with a particular project? How did you meet them?

For me, writing is an ongoing challenge. I've always known I wanted to be a writer, but didn't take care of business in school in my early years. I got serious when I was a college student, taking English to refresh myself and taking several literature and writing classes. Mainly, I am a math person, so sometimes I think I'm writing correctly, when the editor tells me this is wrong or that is wrong. In general, writing is a challenge. Right now, although I'm almost finished with my book manuscripts, the confidence is not there because I feel something is missing. I think I might be having problems with background, for example. I'm studying *The Craft of Writing Science Fiction That Sells* by Ben Bova and hope that helps. I also get tips from my Wednesday evening Writer's Call with Terrie Relf. It's interesting listening to the advice of editors like Relf, Tyree Campbell, and Theresa Santitoro. Other writers in the group also offer great pointers and ideas. As for meeting my challenges, I just keep plugging away at improving my writing.

11. Are you currently, or have you ever, been in a writing group? Your thoughts?

Yes. In 1981 I was briefly in the African American writing group headed by Rob Penney in Pittsburgh in the early eighties. Unknown to me, Penney and Wilson had founded the Pittsburgh theater group I had quit. I was also in an online haibun writers group and two Yahoo writers groups (one for scifaiku and one for African

American writers.) I have also had some creative writing classes. I think it's good to mingle with people, see their views, and fish for ideas. Plus, it's good that others can see what is wrong with your writing that you cannot see. I'm too much of a loner and benefit from the social contact.

12. I'd love to hear about your networking, marketing, and promotional experiences - including tips for other writers.

My networking experience started back in the 80's with Marge Simon and Janet Fox. Marge was the editor of *Star*Line* and Janet (RIP) was editor of *Scavenger's Newsletter*. They gave me lots of encouragement and offered markets for me to send my work.

Thanks to the Internet, I now have Twitter, Instagram, and Facebook. I fondly remember when I first got on MySpace, thanks to the urging of my writer niece Lorrie Irby Jackson and supervisor Melanie Lamanna. When I finally decided to get on the site, I got upset that some stranger asked to friend me. It didn't take long for me to discover that being on MySpace was a good way to get readers. I was further inspired after friending aspiring singers such as Jessie J and Nadina, and editors like James Baker of Pro Mart (now Alban Lake) and J Erwine of Namadic Delirium Press, and seeing them striving for success. The young fan who sent me a message also reinforced my belief in Social Networking as a marketing tool.

I get lots of promoters who offer their services. I specifically like Joey Pinkney, and Faydra Deon. Pinkney is always promoting somebody's book on

Twitter. I also like how Marge, Rhonda Parrish, Tyree, J Alan Erwine, Alban Lake, and yourself do what you can to promote writers. I like social networking because the more friends you get, the higher the probability of getting a publisher and agent as a friend. It's also where potential fans and readers can be found. So, I'd recommend any new writer to make social networking a part of his or her writing life. You don't have to live on it, like many people do, but it is important, if you want to get your name out there.

13. If you're a fiction writer, who are your favorite characters? How did they come into being, and what do you love - or loathe - about them?

I had a story called "The He-man Superheroes Club" published in two publications. The characters were myself and my friends. I liked the characters because, although they had supernatural powers, they were human with all the human weaknesses. I also remember that although I had some abilities they didn't have, they also had some that I didn't. I usually have women characters who are angelic in nature.

One of my characters is taken from a girl I had a crush on in grade school named Jenny. She was a great singer and once taught our sixth grade music class. Thinking about her, I've put a character in my Phenoms manuscript named Siren who can sing all your troubles away.

14. If you're a poet, what forms do you love?

I think one of my weaknesses as a poet is not knowing forms that well. I mostly like haiku and haibun because as I said before, I can feel the images of the poem. I love how my friend Lenard D. Moore performs his haiku and poems with rhythm and style. I still love the poems "Annabell Lee" and "The Raven" by Poe. I have not mastered how to rhyme, but I like that form as well. I guess I can say that the ballade is another favorite form, though I'm not that knowledgeable about it.

15. Anything else you'd like to add that I haven't asked?

Yes, I just want to add that many times, it seems like other things can get in the way of one's writing, such as sickness. It is also true that no matter the situation and how bad the person might feel, when the writer plunges into writing, they get so carried away that nothing can seem to get in the way of their creativity. I also want to add that I have a huge library and besides the book by Bova, some of my other favorite writing books are *Prentice-Hall Handbook for Writers*, edited by Leggett, Mead, and Charvat, *On Being A Writer*, edited by Bill Strickland, *The Haiku Handbook* by William J. Higginson with Penny Harter, and *Science Fiction: What It's All About* by Sam J. Lundwall.

Thank you very much, Terrie, for interviewing me.

BIO; Francis Wesley Alexander is a prostate cancer survivor. At present, the effects of high blood pressure and sugar diabetes are slowing him down, but he still gets enjoyment out of caring for his one kitten and four cats, surfing the Internet, eating, exercising, and writing,

writing, writing. Currently, his work can be found in *Fantasy Short Stories Book Two, Bloodbond, Martian Wave, Disturbed, Anatomy of Hate Anthology,* and *Illumen.*

Edited by Tyree Campbell

The Atomic Age brought with it many wonders and great strides forward. It also brought nuclear war. We often forget how many nuclear warheads are still scattered about our world, and how many countries are still trying to make their own. What would happen to ordinary people if one fell without warning? Follow along in the lives of different people as they move through the drop of a nuclear bomb—before, during, and after the fall. See their lives before the flash, their reactions when the mushroom cloud rises, and how the survivors struggle on.

Available at www.irbstore.com, at Barnes and Noble, and on Amazon.com!

Or just use the order form at the back of this book!

On Xereon
John Grey

I dream and I walk
but in no particular order.
And the landscapes vary little,
though sometimes,
the valleys are the heights,
the heights, the valleys.

The dome door opens
like the mind's French windows,
and there's children playing
in the yard
or capturing small reptiles
by the curling streams
or watching a banchuck
nibble the grasses
or a praylix munching on a banchuck.

So many dawn calls,
from a repercheek seeking a mate
to the zig-zig choir
of the benetrils,
always heard, seldom seen,
and the handirk strutting
across the silicone highway
daring a dot-car to run over him.

Farther afield,
the three-pronged wapari are on the move.
On the rugged hills,
cream-coated diaxils step
dainty as ballerinas
from rock to rock.

In rising sun,
mountains reveal themselves
from summit down.
A lake glistens, as purple
as the surrounding soil.
Horizon light streams yellow, blue and red.

I'm curled up in bed
or I stroll toward the forest,
always breathing fake air
but with true visions.

Choosing a Mate
John Grey

Unnoticed in the hubbub of the store,
of loud oaths and smutty jokes,

one brand new android
silently approaches—

just we two, content, man and machine,
already happy to be together,
no need to speak
though she knows every word there is.

Edited by Tyree Campbell

FEATURED POET:
E. P. Fisher

IN MY CENTURY

In my century, beast & angel fed
On two sides of the brain. Thought was taboo;
Astrology triumphed over logic.
Books went unread; bread & circuses
Were passed off as high civilization.
Cell-line assemblies since Adam & Eve,
Cloned in a test-tube overnight, helped spawn
A gargantuan form of vegetable life
Subject to the endless cycles of rise & fall
In the cataclysmic rhythms of fate.

While others shuddered & spoke with stunned grief
At the nightmare shambles of history,
Oligarchs conspired with assassins
To rule from the shadows with an iron fist.
War-mongers were admired, peacemakers mocked.
Robot zombie armies roamed the streets
As regression to barbarism took hold.
Torn between sudden shock & amnesia,
The helpless were callously swept aside
And the innocent annihilated.

At war with both sides of the heart, justice
Became a kind of fraud, freedom a farce.
Science held a close-out sale on poetry

And child's-play fell prey to the bottom-line.
Body & soul, broadcast live by cathode-ray,
Bounced off the ionosphere night & day.
The death-making machinery of greed
Rocked the headlines with cascading zeroes—
Electronic-transfer of lead into gold
In the greenback columns of boom & bust!

Democracy became its opposite,
Vanishing into skyscraper ruin & smog,
While the pyramid schemes of left & right
Seized the apparatus of the state
And the future collapsed of its own dead weight.
Split-hairs triggered off a chain-reaction
Building up toward doomsday in crisis-mode.
Everything we thought we knew proved false,
While those who hated the truth, would not rest
Till no one was left who dared to dream.

Edited by Tyree Campbell

GYRO

In those days we believed the universe
was full of holes—
Holes into which light itself escaped into
nowhere & deep-time
Like passageways in the maze where Perseus
pursued the Medusa
Or the maelstrom into which Poe was plunged...

A labyrinth where every stuttering attempt
to say something
Ended up in an incomprehensible paradox;
where every testament,
Every witness to the truth, spiraled into
nothingness
And was utterly destroyed...

A dangerous place with something unspeakable
at its center,
Where even advanced mathematics broke down;
A crack in the mute mirror of meaning,
a metaphor for doom
Whispering your name & mine.

And so we settled on the image of stardust
beginnings,
A wrinkle in the eternal here & now which,
like all earthly adventures,
Starts with a symbol, a single grain of sand,
a sign in the sky
And ends in a tumbling hourglass, a scene
from the vast Sahara...

An odyssey blinking over a gulf, a *terra incognita*
of the mind

Taking a blind, circuitous route along the umbra of the moon;
A spectacle red-shifted, in eclipse, dancing around the pupil
Of the dark-adapted eye.

Edited by Tyree Campbell

THE ANATOMY OF SHADOW

The mind is a 'round thing' like the moon
Floating above this place of broken bones,
Orphic in aspect, a mythic orb—
The hollow-eyed Golgotha of the head
And disembodied island of the dead...

The melancholy earth, a four-cornered room
The wind blows through, where the body stoops & bends,
Elbowing out of the womb on phantom-limbs—
Marrow wedded to the suffering soul
Fettered & knitted to sinew & sense.

The animal brain, inhabited by dreams,
Imagines its circumference everywhere—
Time's empty objects thrown up on a screen!
A convoluted cloud, a labyrinth
Whose center keeps its secret like a sphinx.

The pharaoh in X-rays, leans in a fog—
Ghost-image on a photographic plate
Entombed among relics for eternity;
His crooked finger, pointing to a star,
Reconnects circle & square.

Under the trampling of bygone armies
The dead lie quiet: as history's giant stones
Grind the tyrant-Minotaur his bread—
Chalk dust & scattered, rusting iron;
Dice rolled in a game of empires & thrones.

O nameless face the rain has washed away,
Caress this nothingness, this naked ache!
O iris rapt in halos, where chaos waits,

Whisper a prayer, blow out love's candle-flame,
Undress my flesh & lie down in my bones...

Edited by Tyree Campbell

The JD DeHart Page

Insect Dilemma

It is all fine until we get to the pearly gates
and then what we do if the great announcer
is not like us?
We like to picture the angels and their
heavenly lot with faces like ours, but what if
we peer over the gavel and see an alien face?
Will we stand and answer for each careless
movement of our heel, each crushing of carapace
and smashing of stray spider?

Natural Sunlight

It finally burned out, of course
but then all physical elements eventually
deconstruct, reconstruct – that is the eventual
path, the cycle one studies
Now see the colorful pictures in a textbook,
the bright azure arrows swiftly dodging,
one step to the next –
that was how it was, they say, when
the people no longer needed sunglasses
The brightest of our minds (no pun intended)
study the changes carefully by candlelight
listening to the approach of the edge of night,
the nocturnal creatures lapping and churning.

Running Away
Roger Singer

Open boxcars
men failed at chance
broken families
seasons to forget
miles separate the pain
turned up collars
faded jeans
empty pockets
soft eyes
yesterdays meal
from garbage cans
behind a diner
at a river town

bayous and bridges
sand and deserts
push on engines
running hot
grease and creosote
luck long gone
past cemeteries where
worn shoes belong

as iron wheels
create the motion
of leaving something
behind.

Edited by Tyree Campbell

Cherry Wine
Avra Margariti

We're picnicking under the park's biggest oak tree,
nitpicking all the ways I fall short in this relationship.
Spread out on our gingham blanket
in no particular order: soft cheese,
artisan prosciutto, crackers, cherry wine,
my bloody, rare heart.
Witches were hanged from this tree,
you tell me, feeding
me an olive: not the briny flesh, but the grooved stone.
Down in the river, girls were drowned.
They say the silty banks still sing their
sultry gurgling lullaby.
We should go there, you say,
drunk on heartblood wine.
The water's nice this time of year.
Under the park's saddest oak tree, I wonder:
Will you quench my thirst
or will you push me under?

Afterlife
Peter Roberts

by the dismal, dim light
of the burnt brown moon
we go flower sailing.

pale petals part:
stars rain down
to fill empty fields.

now bathed in the glow,
we plunge, naked, below
the shimmering surface.

diving like dolphins,
swimming like stingrays,
purposeless, pausing only

at reefs & atolls,
where we rest & wrestle
amid broken-glass colors.

it all seems so real,
like anything real:

as real as everything,
as real as us,

as real as nothing,
as real as death…

Edited by Tyree Campbell

Rue d'Auseil
DJ Tyrer

Across the dark river
Over a ponderous bridge of dark stone
Hand clamped over mouth, nose
To stifle the malodorous river smell
Along narrow cobbled streets
The way growing steeper and steeper
Up steps carved stair-like in cliff
Till I reach the lofty, ivy-clad wall
That blocks it at the end
Here can be heard strange music
The peculiar, plaintive sound of a viol
Escaping from a gable window high above
The music of a furtive, secretive man
The music of Erich Zann
Louder and louder
Wilder and wilder
The viol shrieks and whines
The screech fills the street
Echoes down the Rue d'Auseil
Echoes down to the filthy river far below
Wilder and wilder
Louder and louder
The viol shrieks and whines
Calling out to far galaxies
Reaching out across the void
The tune overpowers space-time
Louder and louder
Wilder and wilder
The viol shrieks and whines
The musician keeps on playing
Despite being claimed by death
The tune possessing him wholly

I turn and run
Flee the peculiar sound of the viol
Flee the bulging dead eyes
Flee the tune-tainted Rue d'Auseil
Back down the steps
And across the bridge
Back to the world of light and life

Edited by Tyree Campbell

Witch Night
DJ Tyrer

The moon looks away
In sardonic sympathy
As the witches take flight
Sailing through the dreamy astral
Dispensing nightmares and delights
To sleeping souls
Cursing those who crossed them
Rewarding lovers and friends
A strange shadow across the sky
Swooping and sweeping
Down into dark hollows
Where noisome things collect
Waiting to be transformed
Transmogrified into gallant lovers
Before the sun begins to bleed
Its insinuation upon the horizon
And, the witches must return
To bodies sleeping, soulless
On rough and lumpy beds
To live lives devoid of glamour
Unlike their nocturnal ride
Through the torrid sea of dream

The City Built on Ashes
Edward Hickcox

The City of Splendor
Soaring beside the Sea
Astride mighty waterways
All roads leading hence
Capital.
Fortress.
Monument.

From Monument Heights
I am watching the city burn
and smoke and burn.
Madness runs in the streets
Pillaging for goods
While homes crash to ashes.
Fleeing madly for the bridges
Already fallen,
And turning to face the fire.

The city's great cavalry
Ragtag with survivors
Themselves survivors
Reins taut
Eyes rolling
Rearing in the smoke
Hooves smoking in the embers
Wheels at the city center
To make their last stand
Their city already lost.

The mighty horde master
Born under the sign of war
Watches the city burn
Watches his hordes flood the streets
Breaking upon the militia
Washing them away
And flowing on.
The horde master smiles.

I watch and smile as well
Not from pleasure
But from the knowledge
That this city
Has burned
Before
And always
It grows back
Stronger than ever.

Virgo's in Valhalla
Deborah Guzzi

Thunder rolls and rides a black-hearted sky
as in days-gone-by,
In Thor's abode live Valkyries, such as I,
as in days gone-by.

These shield maidens bring Norse heroes to
Valhalla's hall;
Valhalla's Virgo's loft those who die,
as in days-gone-by.

Valkyries judge each fallen warriors and herald
them on high.
Today, as ever, Odin's einherjar rise,
as in days-gone-by.

Virgo's are Valkyries; they champion each
hopeless cause.
Ever lifting, ever striving, they will rise,
as in days-gone-by.

With fire and fidelity each Virgo flames,
she is bold and untamed
but, you can always trust a Virgo not to lie,
as in days-gone-by.

Edited by Tyree Campbell

Origami
Brian Rosenberger

True art demands sacrifice.

She bends and bends, muscles straining
till she hears
The audible crack of bones.
It's one of her favorite sounds, better than laughter,
Better than her cat, Dante's purr,
Better than the sound of birds in the early morning,
Serving as her alarm clock. Annoying but much better than an actual alarm.
The sound echoes in her modest studio/warehouse/home.
Blood pools on the plastic tarp.
The concrete floor slightly stained from past works.
Now, she's more careful, more cautious.
Less cleanup.

Petite, 5' 4" in heels at best,
She's as sinewy as a greyhound, strong as an American Pit.
All muscle. Four days at the gym. Sometimes five.
Not just exercise. A religion.
Her bark is a whisper.
Her bite, a symptom of her desire.

Art, all she desires.
She pushes. She pulls. And when her muscles fail,

She has her tools, a mallet, a hammer.
Sometimes a cleaver, a chisel, a saw.

She soothes her aches, her pains in a bath
With Epsom salts, a glass or two or three of red wine,
And scented candles. Butterscotch her current favorite.
She sips and soaks, thinking of her current work of art,
Thinking of the next.

A Wolf Walks into a Bar
Avra Margariti

You say you're not broken yet
but cracks are doomed to
spread.
And you might wear the sheepskin
I made for you like it's
superglued to your skin,
but the other wolves recognize you as
one of their own.
You can draw roses on every piece of paper
but you'll still get a hundred tiny
papercuts from the black-ink
thorns.

Your creators must be so proud.
They made you perfect in their own twisted
image.
That's why you're on a mission
to unmake yourself just as
perfectly.

Who?

Brian Rosenberger lives in a cellar in Marietta, GA and writes by the light of captured fireflies. He is the author of As the Worm Turns and three poetry collections. He is also a featured contributor to the Pro-Wrestling literary collection, Three-Way Dance, available from Gimmick Press.

Jen Sexton-Riley says: I am a Clarion West 2018 graduate and a SFWA associate member. My short fiction has appeared in Daily Science Fiction and The Colored Lens, and is scheduled to appear in both the spring 2020 issue of Ghostlight: The Magazine of Terror and an upcoming urban fantasy anthology titled "Class and Magical Sass" edited by Corrugated Sky Publishing.

My nonfiction work has appeared in VIA Magazine, Inside Kung Fu Magazine, Cape Cod Magazine, Chatham Magazine, and Qi Journal. I am a former contributing editor at Peripheral

Surveys and at Mary Engelbreit's Home Companion magazine. I am currently a staff writer and proofreader at an independently-owned weekly newspaper in a seaside New England village.

Rachel Rodman (www.rachelrodman.com) writes fairy tales, food poetry, and popular science. Her work has appeared at Fireside Fiction, Daily Science Fiction, Dreams & Nightmares, and elsewhere

Simon Kewin is the author of over 100 published short and flash stories. His works have appeared in Analog, Nature, Daily Science Fiction, Abyss and Apex and many more. He is also the author of a growing number of novels. He lives deep in the English countryside. Find him at simonkewin.co.uk.

DJ Tyrer is the person behind *Atlantean Publishing*, was placed second in the 2015 Data Dump Award for Genre Poetry, and has been published in *The Rhysling Anthology 2016*, issues of *Cyaegha, Frostfire Worlds, The Horrorzine, Illumen, Outposts of Beyond, Scifaikuest, Sirens Call, Star*Line, Tigershark* and *The Yellow Zine*, and online at *Grievous Angel, Lonesome October,* and *Three Drops from a Cauldron*, as well as releasing several chapbooks, such as *The Tears of Lot-49*.

DJ Tyrer's website is at https://djtyrer.blogspot.co.uk/

The Atlantean Publishing website is at https://atlanteanpublishing.wordpress.com/

E. P. Fisher says: I taught high school English in Uganda as a Peace Corps volunteer, and worked for 30 years as a play therapist and adventure-based counselor with special needs children.

I hold a bachelor's degree in Literature and the doctorate in Psychology.

Previous credits include four books and publication in over 100 small college journals & little magazines, including *The Writer, The Lyric, Chaffin, Illuminations, Crucible, Licking River, Alembic, Leading Edge, Listening Eye, Sanskrit, Saranac, Urthona, Ibbetson Street, Nassau* and *Wisconsin Reviews*. Pushcart nominee and winner of New York Poetry Forum competitions. Other works appeared in Johns Hopkins University Press & Association for the Study of Play.

Daniel C. Smith has published dozens of stories, articles, reviews and poems in the genres of science fiction and horror. His speculative poetry has received an honorable mention the year's Best of Fantasy and Horror and has also been included in several anthologies, including *Changes, Wondrous Web Worlds*, and *Dwarf Stars*. his first two collections of short fictions, Nano-Bytes and 3 of a Perfekt Pear, are available from Nomadic Delirium Press <nomadicdeliriumpress.com>.

John Grey is an Australian poet, US resident. Recently published in That, Muse, Poetry East and North Dakota Quarterly with work upcoming in South Florida Poetry Journal, Hawaii Review and the Dunes Review.

Deborah Guzzi writes full time. She was a candidate for both the Science Fiction Poetry Association's Rhysling Award & the Pushcart Prize. Her book, *The Hurricane,* published by Prolific Press, is now available. Her poetry appears in Heroic Fantasy Quarterly, Eye to the Telescope, Bete Noir, Liquid Imagination, Illumen, Literary Hatchet, Zetetic, and Silver Blade among others in the USA.

Order Your Books Today!

Book	Price	Amount	Total
Illumen Subscription			
One Year	$29.00		
Two Years	$56.00		
Adventures of Colo Collins	$10.00		
Vow of Blood Collection	$42.99		
When the Mushrooms Come	$5.95		
		Subtotal	$
		Shipping	
		1 book	$3.80
		2 books	$4.35
		3 books	$4.90
		4 or more books	$6.00
		Final Total	$

Name: _____
Address: _____
City: _____
State: _____
Zip: _____
Phone: _____
Date: _____

Checks or money orders need to be made out to Alban Lake Publishing.

For Credit Card Orders:
Card #: _____
Exp. Date: _____
Security Code: _____
Date: _____
Signature: _____

Alban Lake Publishing
P.O. Box 141
Colo, IA 50056-014
515-357-8910 (texts welcome)
albanlake@yahoo.com
Website: www.albanlakepublishing.com

www.ingramcontent.com/pod-product-compliance
Lightning Source LLC
Chambersburg PA
CBHW052122110526
44592CB00013B/1719